BRUSH UP YOUR GRAMMAR

A Pocket Guide for Professional Writers and Speakers.

Compiled by Caroline Davis

First printing   1980
Second printing 1981
Third printing   1981
Fourth printing   1982

ISBN 0 9507623 1 8

Copies may be obtained
from the publishers
or bookshops
@ **£2.50** incl. postage.

Solo Publishing
105 Great North Road, Eaton Socon, St. Neots, Cambs PE19 3EL.

Designed and printed by **Soloprint Limited**

ACKNOWLEDGEMENTS

To Mr. J. W. Clifton of the Queen's English Society for careful vetting and criticism.

To the Daily Telegraph for the Holland cartoons.

To the Telegraph and Miss Tracy for a shortened version of her article.

FOREWORD

Many text-books have been published for children who are learning to write, or for scholars who want to know the finer points of language. Ours is something different: a booklet to jog the minds of writers and speakers whose business is words, but who all their lives may have made some small errors of grammar without being aware of it. In fact, most of us probably have blind spots of this sort. These small errors are so common and so familiar that they sound all right to those who use them. Why then are they wrong?

Well, there are rules to grammar as to any other subject, and the correct version sounds so much better to those who know them. Also, if you speak or write for the public you have a responsibility to the language.

One of the casualties of the permissive age has been our once-careful English speech. But now there is a move afoot to halt its deterioration. We are delighted, and are anxious to add our contribution to this. We hope this light-hearted booklet will interest and amuse as well as being of some practical value.

Most of the sentences here criticised have been heard on the radio recently, or read in books of fiction or non-fiction, all by good writers.

So please . . . brush up your grammar a little.

Caroline Davis B.A.

INDEX

PRONOUNS . . . MISUSE OF 'I' AND 'WE'

What is wrong with this sentence?

Oh that the ship would carry you and I to some foreign shore!

The ship can't carry I; it carries **ME**. Putting any other word in front does not change this.

Although our nouns don't have different cases, there is one group of words that does: pronouns.

Subjective	Objective	Possessive
I	me	my or mine
you	you	your, yours
he	him	his
she	her	her, hers
it	it	its
we	us	our, ours
they	them	their, theirs

Verbs, except intransitive ones (such as go, come, look, weep, happen etc.), govern an object. If the object is a pronoun it must be in the objective case, whether it is the only object or one of several.

Take the child and me with you, please.
It was wrong to blame her and him.
The edict affects our neighbours and us.

This is a shocking sentence:

There were incipient symptoms which worried we medical men.
(from a Conference Sketch)

Nothing that comes after the pronoun — whether it be an adverb, descriptive phrase, or a whole additional sentence — changes its case from the objective.

Our captors treated the Germans and us as though we were not enemies but friends.
The crowd cheered the winners and us losers equally.

PREPOSITIONS

It wasn't fair to leave so much responsibility to you and I.

Prepositions should also be followed by the objective case form. This is obvious with a single preposition: to me, with me, after me etc.

Less obvious, but still required, when there are two or more objects: to you and me, with him and me, after them and us.

The prepositions in most common use are:
above — after — at — before — below — between — by — except — for — from — in — into — inside — of — on — onto — outside — over — to — towards — through — throughout — under — with — within — without

They gave the flowers to Ruth, Joan and me.
Johnnie's teacher is pleased with his brother and him.
Privileges were taken away from me and her.
The good feeling persisted inside them as well as us.

When 'but' and 'save' are used in the prepositional sense of 'except' the same rule applies:

All but him managed to escape.
The favours went to all save us two.
It doesn't concern anyone but me.

Here are two examples that are bad, bad, bad.

The Americans doing that makes it difficult for we in this country.

(heard on 'Any Questions')

There is a tall, brown-eyed brunette in Paris who is an example to all we Britons.

(quoted in Sunday Telegraph magazine)

SINGULAR POSSESSIVES

This is probably the most common error of all.

What is wrong with this sentence?

Anyone who'd believe that needs to have their heads examined.
(from a novel)

'Anyone' has only one head, so it should read *his head*, not *their*. 'Anyone needs' is obviously singular.

The rule:

Someone, anyone, no-one, somebody, anybody, nobody are all singular, and should always be followed by the singular possessive 'his' or 'her'. Not by the plural *their*.

Less obviously, 'everyone' and 'everybody' are also singular because they mean 'each body' or 'each person'.

If anyone misses the train it is his own fault.
Customs kept the whole party waiting because someone had lost her keys.
No one ever protested his innocence more loudly.
Everybody must have some idea of his own strength.
In an instant everyone on the veranda leapt to his feet.
There was a crowd and I thought, "Somebody must have hurt himself".

A pronoun or verb referring to one of the above should also be singular.

If anybody knows the answer he mustn't tell.
There's a frightful draught. Who has left his window open?

If the subject is plural, then use plural throughout, including the verb.

How many have left their windows open? or
How many of you have left your windows open?
Many people like keeping their coats on indoors.
All in the audience may wear their coats. or
All of you may wear your coats.

THE VERB 'TO BE'

What is wrong here?

Of course it's him. It must be him. It was him yesterday. It has to be him.

The verb 'to be' is irregular in many languages.

I am	you are	he is
we are	you are	they are
I was	you were	he was
I shall be		
I have been etc.		

This verb can never take an object in any of its forms. It should be followed by the subjective pronouns: I, he, she, we, they, and not by the objective ones: me, him, her, us or them.

It is I. It is she. It was he who said it.
It must be we who are chosen.
It wasn't he (whom) the child wanted.

If the sentence sounds stilted it is often better to rephrase it.

We must be the ones chosen.
He wasn't the one the child wanted.

Note 1. 'It's me', although not correct, is so commonly used that it is now accepted as an idiom of the language.

Note 2. When one is writing dialogue rules do not apply. One must interpret the character as he or she would normally speak. It is one of the chief characteristics.

The adjectives 'idiomatic' and 'colloquial' and the noun 'vernacular' are applied to common expressions in ordinary speech, and these are acceptable in dialogue.

SPLIT INFINITIVES

But not a very serious fault:

. . . said she is to formally request the British Olympic Association to consider alternative sites for the games.
(from Telegraph news column)

The infinitive of a verb is the root plus the word 'to'. To be, to have, to know, to care.

If an adverb is put between these, the infinitive is said to be split.

to everlastingly grieve
to foolishly hope

Split infinitives are usually awkward. But they are preferable to

      a) a real ambiguity
      b) a patent artificiality (Fowler p. 558)

Sometimes they even make the meaning clearer. These, for instance, might be allowed:

intended to better equip the successful candidates
to more thoroughly pursue the subject
to mortally wound his opponent

Other avoiding constructions are correct but very formal:

intended the better to equip candidates
the more thoroughly to pursue the subject

In a compound verb (to be known), it is not a split infinitive if the 'to' and 'be' are not separated.

to be really understood
to be mortally wounded
to be everlastingly grieving

HANGING PARTICIPLES

Referring to your letter you do not state . . .

You don't mean that he is referring to his letter but that you are.

Referring to your letter I notice that you do not state . . .

The 'ing' form of a verb is a participle:
having, feeling, knowing, remembering

Participles require subjects. The subject of 'referring' is I. I am referring to it.

Sitting on the balcony the evening breeze made us cool.

It is not the evening breeze that is sitting on the balcony but you.

Sitting on the balcony we were cooled by the evening breeze.

Looking at the national exchange rate, the fall in the pound was inevitable.

There is no subject for 'looking'. It could read:
In view of the national exchange rate, the fall etc.

Being the queen, nobody asked her for her credentials.
Being the queen, she was not asked for her credentials.

This is an extremely common error, especially in formal and official papers.

This grammatical error is most often used with the past participle:
having had, having felt, having overlooked

It is good that the Minister made the position of Government so clear. Having done so, there can now be no going back.
(Politician speaking on radio)

This should be:
Having done so he can not now go back. or
Now that he has done so, there can be no going back.

MORE HANGING PARTICIPLES

These are all too common. Here are some more examples, with suggested corrections underneath.

Having finished his work, there was still time for a quick game.
Having finished his work, he still had time for a quick game.

Having said all that, let me say at once . . .
Having said all that, I must say at once . . .

Having waited about twenty minutes, a large herd of elephants appeared.
When we had waited about twenty minutes, a large herd of elephants appeared.

Having decided to run away, it was only natural that the child should have disappeared.
Having decided to run away the child disappeared, which was only natural.

Having said goodbye to her parents, they didn't wait to see her onto the train.
Having said goodbye to her parents, she was glad they didn't wait . . .

Or these could be reversed with the subject in front.
The girl, having said goodbye to her parents, was glad they didn't wait.

Usually diagrams were shown with slides but, having no electricity, projections were out.
. . . as we had no electricity, projections were out.
or: . . . having no electricity we couldn't use projections.

Since even the best writers sometimes fall into this trap, it is perhaps wise to avoid starting sentences with 'having' and write, for example:

As the child had decided to run away . . .
(which also sounds less stilted)

Since they had already said goodbye, her parents didn't wait.

DOUBLE PAST TENSES

Two past tenses are too many.
I would have liked to have gone.

Either of the following is correct:
I would have liked (in the past) **to go.** or
I would like (now) **to have gone** (in the past).
i.e. **I wish now that I had gone.**

DOUBLE PASSIVE VERBS

Now that the whole is attempted to be systematised . .

This is bad and awkward:
Now that there is an attempt to systematise the whole . . .

DOUBLE NEGATIVES

These are also wrong:
I shouldn't wonder if it didn't turn to snow.
I shouldn't wonder if it turned (or did turn) **to snow.**

I don't really know what people get from reading all these books; not often, I don't think, a greater familiarity with the writers.
(not often, I think, . . .)

DOUBLE COMPARATIVES

I was more happier at school than at any time since.
I was happier . . .

DOUBLE SUPERLATIVES

They were the most happiest days of my life.
They were the happiest days . . .

NEGATIVE OF 'USED TO'

The negative of 'used to' is 'used not to'.
I used to be afraid of thunderstorms.
I used not to mind them so much.
Used you not to write poetry?

THE EXPRESSION 'ALL RIGHT'

She wanted to know if it was alright to mix litres with gallons.

Almost, although, already, albeit, and Almighty are all correct words.

But there is no such word as *alright.*

This is two words: **all right..**

Please remember that alright is alwrong!

Altogether is one word:

The result was altogether satisfactory.

But all together has a slightly different meaning.

All together we accomplished the deed.

THE IMPERSONAL 'ONE'

The impersonal 'one' should be followed by the possessive one's . . . not by 'his'.

It is easy for one to lose one's way.

But used more than two or three times 'one' becomes tiresome:

When one sets out on one's travels, one often finds one's fellow travellers not at all congenial to one's moods.

This is a trap, because you can't change over to 'he'.

Better begin again:

When you set out on your travels you often find . . . or **When a person sets out on his travels he often finds . . .**

(The use of 'one' became fashionable in Victorian times, when too many 'I's' were considered to be in bad taste).

THE WORD 'BETWEEN'

Is this all right?

You could make a colourful flower border by putting a white one between every pink.
(from an article on gardening)

'Between implies two objects. (Latin: bis = two).

The white has a pink on each side and is therefore between two pinks.

Dusk comes between the day and the night.

Between you and me there must always be affection.

When there are more than two objects the word should be 'among' or 'in the midst of'.

Portia's suitors had to choose among three caskets.
(or 'one out of three')

The old lady could not decide among all the gifts on the tree.

There he stood in the midst of the children.

Note: You choose between one thing **and** another, not **or** another.

The choice is between glorious death and shameful life.

THE WORD 'ALTERNATIVE'

'Alternative' also implies two objects (alter = other)

'A pair of possibilities from which only one can be selected' (Fowler)

Since he refused to accept the committee's decision he had no alternative but to resign.

She didn't want to go to Spain but there was an alternative. She could go to Italy.

(Not 'another alternative' since there is only one other)

If there are more than one:

She didn't want to go to Spain but there were several other possibilities.
(or choices, or countries to choose from etc.).

(But this rule is apparently being relaxed to allow more than two alternatives.)

THE WORD 'LIKE'

What is wrong with this sentence?

London needs another office block like it needs the plague.
(from a news commentary)

'Like' requires a direct object.

It was just like summer.
Sarah is like her mother.
He talks like an expert.
You, like me, are disappointed.
Like them, Anthony was an insatiable gambler.

It should *never* be followed by a verbal phrase:

. . . cakes like Mother used to make . . .
. . . cakes like the ones Mother used to make . . .

It's true, like I always told you.
It's true as I always told you.

It wasn't like her to do like she did.
. . . as . . . or . . . what . . . she did.

(The *verb* 'like' is a different matter. You can like to go. etc.).

THE WORD 'THAN'

'Than' does not take an object, but the two words compared should be in the same case, whether subjective or objective.

He is much taller than I. (both subjective)
You love him more than me. (both objective)

Mentally putting in the understood word shows at once what the case should be. In the first sentence 'than I am', in the second, 'than you love me'.

It was to me rather than (to) him that the criticism referred.
You treat her worse than I (do).

But the sense is different if you say:

You treat her worse than (you treat) me.

THE WORD 'UNIQUE'

'Unique' comes from the Latin 'unus' meaning 'one'.

It means unmatched, unequalled, only one of its kind.

It can not be qualified into *rather unique* or *very unique*.

There was only one Anna Pavlova. She was unique.

If there is more than one, an object may be 'rare', 'special', or 'exceptional'.

However, 'almost unique' is permissible.

'KIND' AND 'SORT'

How often do you hear:
You don't find these kind of things any more.

The speaker has started with the plural 'these' and thinks there must be another plural, and so puts it on 'thing'.

But 'this' belongs to 'kind', and not to 'things'. Therefore it must read either **this kind of thing,** or **these kinds of thing.**

The former sounds better and can refer to either singular or plural objects.

this sort of person
people of this kind (or sort).

'Kinds' is best used in expressions like 'all kinds', 'several kinds', 'many kinds'.

The child has many different kinds of toy.
He will succeed in all kinds of pursuit.

'LESS' AND 'FEWER'

The less people involved in this the better.
(from a radio commentary)

The difference between 'less' and 'fewer' is the difference between a single substance and several objects: how much. . . less; how many. . . fewer. The common error is to use 'less' when 'fewer' would be correct; never the other way around. I.e., you hear *there were less cups than saucers*, but never *I want fewer sugar in my tea*.

So it is less in amount but fewer in number. 'Less milk', but 'fewer bottles of milk'.

The fruit made less jam than before.
More rather than less concrete will be needed.
There is less harmony than I could wish.

There were fewer mistakes in his paper.
Fewer boys than last year will go on to university.
There was less noise because there were fewer people in the hall.

'DUE TO' AND 'OWING TO'

Transport to school will be required, due to the distance.
(from a radio discussion)

'Due to' is used much too often. It is permissible only in the sense of 'owed to'. That is, when there is a concrete object or something that can be given or conferred.

Danger money was due to the men on that job.
James guesssed right and the prize is due to him.
Praise is due to the life-saver for his gallant effort.

Otherwise, for an idea or abstraction, it should always be 'owing to', which is used in the sense of 'because of'.

Owing to illness (because of illness) **he was unable to come.**
Owing to the fact that his watch was slow he missed the train.
The sports were cancelled owing to bad weather.
The president was absent owing to circumstances beyond his control.

'AFFECT' AND 'EFFECT'

'Affect' means have an influence on, change.

This will not affect (change) his purpose.
It may seriously affect his health. (change it for better or worse)

'Affect' may also mean to assume, pretend.

He affected a clown's costume.
He affected (pretended) **to be dumb.**

The latter meaning gives affectation, affected (studied display) and sense of artificiality.

'Effect' means bring about, cause, result in.

The drug may effect (bring about) his recovery.
How have you effected the transformation? (caused, completed)

'Effect' as a noun means 'result', 'consequence'.

What effect would it have if you told her?

It also gives the adjective 'effective'.

The lighting was most effective.

'ALLUDE' AND 'ELUDE'

'Allude' means refer indirectly, covertly, and requires 'to' after it.

I allude to what you said this morning.

'Allusion' is an indirect reference.

His story contained an allusion to an old folk tale.

'Elude' means escape from.

She eluded her captors and got quite away.

It gives the adjectives elusive and elusory. (That which we fail to grasp physically or mentally).

'Illusion' means delusion, giving the adjectives illusive, illusory.

SOME REFINEMENTS OF SPEECH

The word 'if' takes the subjunctive form of the verb in these instances:

If I were you . . .
If it were not a fact that . . .
If Mr. Bloggs were to die his children would inherit.

THE GERUND

Usually has a possessive sense:
He didn't like my going.
(not *'me'* going)
The members were uneasy about his being admitted.
(not *'him'* being admitted)

SHALL AND WILL

I shall be away for the next fortnight.
(simple future)
I will do it although I don't want to.
(determination or compulsion)
No one else will want that afterward.
(simple future)
He shall not have a penny from me.
(determination or compulsion)
Note that the meanings are reversed.

The Lord is my shepherd, I shall not want . . .
He shall give His angels charge . . .
(Biblical and poetic)

MAY AND MIGHT

If the weather had not been so bad the number may have been greater.

But the weather was bad, and so the number might have been greater.

The past tense here indicates a greater improbability.

Had it not been for a bit of luck I might not have been acquitted.
(not *'may'*)

He may have taken bribes when he was in college.
(We are making a serious allegation)

He might have taken bribes.

(He could have but did not)

CLICHÉS

by the skin of his teeth
at the end of his tether
right, left, and centre
hook, line, and sinker
in this day and age
no smoke without fire
more in sorrow than in anger
long arm of coincidence
take it in your stride
like a fish out of water
off the deep end
strong as an ox, black as ink, cold as ice

The list is endless. All were good when first used, but their repetition is lazy. A good writer will think up something original.

SIMPLICITY PREFERRED

My first object was to endeavour to ascertain what the others were going to do.
(Heard on The World at One)

Wouldn't '**try to find out**' sound better?

Why not the good Anglo-Saxon word?

sufficient	enough	cease	stop
commence	begin	centre	middle
complete	finish	terminate	end

Ugly expressions (or journalese — a few examples among many)

following on	after	prior to	before
in advance of	before	adverse to	against
subsequent to	after	finalise	complete
previous to	before	in conjunction with	with

Rather pretentious

donation	gift	collation	light meal
apprehension	fear	orientated	oriented
intimidate	frighten	disassociate	dissociate
edifice	building	escalate	increase gradually

FIGURES OF SPEECH

Similes and metaphors are both adornments to prose, describing something by comparing it to something else, or by using words that belong to something else.

The moon broken in pieces in the river . . .
(compared to a broken plate)

It is a simile when the word 'like' is used (similar); otherwise it is a metaphor.

An old, old man with a cart-load of dreams.
The horsechestnut with all its candles lighted.
A woman bearing down on them like a ship in full sail . . .
A girl like a narcissus, bending this way and that in the wind.

MEMORABLE

"He lay back on the long grass and his eyes filled with stars".
(Iris Murdoch)

"A fleet of white ducks lay at anchor, bobbing and dipping . . ."
(Rosamond Lehmann)

"The weeks turn over page by page as a plot turns over in the mind. Months turn over like chapters".
(Sylvia Ashton-Warner)

"A man alone building a house, stirring hope into the concrete mixture, painting the walls with memories".
(Ibid.)

"The little closely-hedged fields jostled each other down to the sea".
(Brackenbury)

"White forms of geese disperse like paper boats with a wind behind them".
(Jacky Gillott)

"Baby rabbits whose white scuts vanished into the bramble patches like blown dandelion clocks".
(Ibid.)

PUNCTUATION . . . THE ERRATIC COMMA

The only punctuation mark with which there is much trouble is the comma. This is used very erratically and usually too much. If it is not needed, leave it out . . . as in a short sentence.

The day was fine and they decided to go out.

Rules are difficult, but here are a few:

Use it before 'and' or 'but' to break up a long sentence.

The menu was large and varied, but no one seemed able to find anything he wanted.

Before and after a quotation:

Jane replied, "I will if you insist", and turned her back.

After an exclamation:

Oh well, perhaps we should tell her after all.

To divide a string of adjectives:

Tall, short, thin, fat, and medium-sized soldiers.

The smooth grey of the beech stem, the silky texture of the birch, and the rugged pine and oak.
(Comma needed before 'and' here, to show that 'silky' does not apply to 'pine and oak').

Before and after an inserted phrase. I.e. the sentence would make perfectly good sense without it.

The children, all except Sarah's, were soaking wet.
(The children were soaking wet).

He was given a choice but, even so, didn't get what he wanted.
(Comma after 'but', not 'choice')

To distinguish a meaning:

John, having drawn attention to the time, called a break.

but **John having drawn attention to the time, the secretary called a break.**
(No comma after John)

DIVIDING WORDS

This is the printer's province, since only he will know when a word over-runs the end of a line and has to be divided. But the author should always check on this in the proofs.

A word should be broken only between syllables, and dividing words into their proper syllables is one of the functions of a good dictionary.

There is one hard and fast rule. Never break the root of a word, but separate it from its ending only.

I.e. endings such as: ing, ed, able, ity etc.

Serv is a root, and makes such words as:

serv/ice, serv/ant, serv/ile, serv/iceable, serv/itude

Cf. lov-ing, plea-sant, plea-sure, rent-ed, dirt-y, cru-elty, reach-ing, trust-ful, point-less etc.

Don't let such horrors appear as:

trus - tworthy	peri - sher
sear - ching	rea - ched
leng - then	streng - then
screwd - river	rem - ember
ano - ther	deligh - ted

What do you suppose he means by "Wasted all afternoon looking for a screwd-river?"

SOME UNGRAMMATICAL SENTENCES FROM RECENT BOOKS, PAPERS AND BROADCASTS

We have decided you must choose one of we three.
(one of us three)
They moved away into the dark, leaving Christopher and I alone.
(leaving me)
As truly as no-one but I shall ever drink from this glass.
(no-one but or except me)
[cf. No-one shall drink but me)
It is people like she who would happily slip back in time.
(people like her)
Her mother bought her the house. Now let she and her husband get on with it.
(let her and her husband)
It was a good chance for Olivier and she to be together.
(chance for her)
Can you imagine how we feel about these large index-linked pensions being financed by all we taxpayers?
(by us taxpayers)
And in who else could she have found so kind a man?
(in whom else)
No—one could come in until he had vetted them.
(vetted him)
Nobody else had such blue water in their pool.
(his or her pool)
Heavens !   Somebody must have cut themselves shaving !
(cut himself)
It would be her who was ill.
(would be she, or She would be the one who was ill)
There were many people coming out, but not her.
(not she; she was not one of them)
He wrote to her saying that, although he was younger than her, he was now head of the family.
(younger than she [was])
There was speculation about him resigning in the next few months.
(about his resigning)

I could approach them quite openly without them noticing.
(without their noticing)
After collecting a fair sum of money the project fell through.
(after we had collected)
After knocking two or three times, a little boy opened the door.
(when we had knocked)

Turning back for a last look, the towers had disappeared.
(when we turned back)
Painting the outside of a third-storey window two years ago, the cradle broke.
(when he was painting)
While sharing measles with my brother James, he told me the story of King Solomon's mines.
(while I was sharing)
How I should have liked you to have been there.
(liked you to be there)
It would have been impossible for it to have been mentioned.
(for it to be mentioned)
To the end of her life she would like to have seen him reinstated.
(would have liked to see)
One can but muse on the lengths she would have had to have gone to achieve a hundred percent.
(she would have had to go)
She went on down between the tea.
(between the rows or the tea bushes)
Forty-five minutes was allowed between each.
(between races, lectures, or whatever the objects were)
The road ran between a cleft on the beach.
(through a cleft)
Stopping for ten seconds between every word to wonder what to say next.
(after every word)
We began to creep forward, pausing between every step to listen.
(after every step, or between steps)
Every kind of drama script has one thing in common.
(all kinds of script have . . .)

No one plant is identical.
(no two plants are identical)
He has made eight films. None of them has been similar.
(similar to what? None of them has been like any other)
Generally speaking each rank stuck together.
(the members of each rank)
I witness the curious interdependence that seems to connect everyone else.
(connect all the others)
They were tiny grey birds with a curved beak.
(several birds would have several beaks)
Some of the houses had broken earthenware pots as a chimney.
(as chimneys)
How silly not to have an electric kettle like I had in the flat.
(as I had, or like the one I had)
Fishing for free advice, like people did at cocktail parties.
(the way people did)

I think you are very snobbish about those kind of people.
(that kind of person or better, people like that)
These kind of men who want power are all alike.
(these men who want power)
It was one of those dry kind of seeds.
(dry kinds of seed)
Many poor girls wed with only confused notions of marriage due to the prudery of their mothers.
(owing to)
This programme is different to any other.
(different from)
In the field to the back of my house all the elms have died.
(in back, or at the back)
Very different to being brought into the world of professionals.
(different from, not to)
Had we not been a compatible team we would not have persisted in our succession of failures.
(persisted after, not persisted in)

On foot the creepers catch your skin and clothes.
(if or when you are on foot . . .)
Seated, the short skirt revealed her legs to the knee.
(when she was seated)
At seven years old ribbons and laces met with my
delighted approval.
(When I was seven)
Unlike most of his forebears soldiering held no
attractions for him.
(Unlike his forebears he was not attracted to)
or (He was unlike his forebears in that soldiering
held . . .)
Both sides must now agree together.
(together is redundant as agree implies two cr more)
It was the beginning of a battle between John and
myself.
(the reflexive is used only in conjunction with its
noun or pronoun: Henry . . . himself; I . . . myself
etc.).
He used to spend so long that his porridge used to
get cold.
(only one 'used to'; his porridge got, or would get,
cold)

More people buy apples than any other fruit.
('more' applies to apples, not people; i.e. people buy
more apples . . .)
The tragedy can still be averted, but so far no one has
shown an inclination to do so.
('to do it' would sound better)
I retain the original letter and for my own records
have kept a copy of the same.
(a copy of it)

A FEW PITFALLS AND PUZZLES
(Selected from Fowler's 'Modern English Usage')

Ago and since
One or the other should be used but not both.
It is barely twenty years ago since it was lost.
He died twenty years ago.
It was twenty years ago that he died.
It is twenty years since he died.

Because
Because is incorrect after 'is' or 'was'.
The reason was because he was going out.
The reason was that he was going out.

Below and under
Below the bridge means farther down the river.
Under the bridge means with it overhead.

Chronic
Means lingering, lasting, long-established.
It does not mean bad, intense, or severe.

Circumstances
Mere situation is expressed by 'in' the circumstances.
Action affected is performed 'under' the circumstances.
In the circumstances in which I found myself . . .
Under the circumstances I decided not to venture.

Collusion
The notion of fraud or underhandedness is essential.
Otherwise the word is 'collaboration'.
Two authors working together in collaboration are not necessarily in collusion.

Comparatively few
Comparatively few people are in the secret.
Not a comparative few or a comparatively few.

Decimate
From the Latin decimus (ten). It means to destroy a

tenth or a proportion of, but not to destroy altogether.

Caesar's army was decimated in the war.

Depends on or upon

It all depends who is going to read the paper.
It all depends on (or upon) who is chosen.

Each

Each is usually singular.
Each of them has a chance to choose.
But here the sense is plural throughout.
They are each of them masters in their own houses.

The possessive is:
A lot of old cats ready to tear out each other's eyes.
(not others')

The expression 'each other'
We each know what the other wants.
(not what each other wants)

Ellipsis

The omission of a needed word or words.
Divorce is on the increase, and broken homes are rising drastically.
(the number of homes)
Brasses shining like a Whitbread's dray horse.
(like those on a horse)

Else

It is easier to recognise someone else's faults than one's own.
(not someone's else)

Greek and Latin plurals

criterion	criteria	medium	media
phenomenon	phenomena	opus	opera
datum	data	genus	genera
candelabrum	candelabra	addendum	addenda

afflatus, apparatus, hiatus, impetus, prospectus, octopus, polypus etc. all form English plurals. Gladioluses is now accepted in place of gladioli.

Hardly and scarcely
These should be followed by 'when' and not by 'than'.

Hardly had he opened the door when the men burst in.

They had scarcely come into bloom when they were picked.

Literally
Means actually. If not true, it is over-emphasis and weakens rather than strengthens the statement.

A battalion crossed the bridge literally on the enemy's shoulders.
(practically, virtually, or almost)

Mixed metaphors

Joining two images which belong to different objects.

"He has buttered his bun and must now lie on it". A famous comedy line.

It's much too early to throw up the sponge when there's already light at the end of the tunnel.

Must and need
The two words go together, one being the negative of the other.

Must it be so? Yes it must. No it need not. Need I do it? No, you need not. Yes you must.

Nouns of multitude
Army, fleet, company, government, crowd etc. may be either singular or plural according to the sense.

The cabinet is divided.
The cabinet are agreed.
The party lost its way.
The crowd lost their hats.

Oblivious
He drove off quite oblivious that any harm had been done.

This should be 'unaware' or 'unmindful.'

He has become oblivious of other people's pain.

Only

Should be put in the right position for the verb it governs.

I saw him only a week ago.

I only saw him and didn't speak to him.

Other, otherwise

No new invention could come in other than through a specific company.

Although the world refused to treat it otherwise than humorously . . .

Palpable

Means touchable, perceptible by touch.

Her attempt at an innocent smile was such a *palpable* failure that she had to laugh at herself.

This should be 'complete' or 'obvious' failure.

Possessive variables

When the final 's' is intrinsic and does not of itself designate a plural, an extra 's' is added for the possessive.

Mr. Jones's cow; Charles's beard; Mrs. Harris's cottage; Iris's letter; The Times's opinion.

But cf. ordinary plurals:

the girls' room; birds' wings; travellers' tales; forces' favourites.

Plural anomalies

Mumps, measles, glanders, innings, corps etc. can be treated as either singular or plural.

The team had a very good innings this morning.

Plural oddities

courts martial	brothers-in-law
bons mots	Lords Justices
A.D.C.s	trade unions
appendices	knights errant

Preposition at end of sentence

This is allowed if it makes for simplicity.

There is no-one to fix the blame on.
It's the only thing I could put up with.
It was the worst fight he ever engaged in.
Insisted with all the eloquence he is master of.

Quantity words

Also singular or plural according to sense.

There is heaps of ammunition.
There are heaps of cups.
There is lots to do.
Lots of people think so.
Half of it is rotten.
Half of them are bad.

Reciprocal and mutual

A road between their two estates would be of mutual benefit.
(a single shared benefit)

If Tom has given a gift to Harry, Harry must give Tom a reciprocal one.
(two separate gifts)

That and which

These are used indiscriminately, but sometimes one sounds better than the other.

The heat is such that it will boil water.
I always buy his books, which have influenced me greatly.

It was the rose whose colour was so perfect.
It was a new book, the title of which was Modern Poetry.

Various

Should not be followed by 'of'.

Not *various of the rooms*, but various rooms of the house.

What (meaning 'that which' or 'those which'.)

May be singular or plural.

What is really at issue is the location.
What is required are three bedrooms.
I have few books and what I have don't help me much.

PAIRS AND SNARES

Words which are often confused
(see also page 31)

afflict	ceremonial	complacent
inflict	ceremonious	complaisant
compose	contemptible	contend
comprise	contemptuous	contest
credible	dependant	derisive
creditable	dependent	derisory
eligible	fatal	forceful
illegible	fateful	forcible
immovable	infer	incredible
irremovable	imply	incredulous
inflammable	insensitive	instil
inflammatory	insentient	inspire
luxuriant	masterful	militate
luxurious	masterly	mitigate
pendant	policy	precipitate
pendent	polity	precipitous
predict	proposal	purport
predicate	proposition	propose
regretful	resource	reverend
regrettable	recourse	reverent
reversal	sensual	triumphant
reversion	sensuous	triumphal

ADDENDUM

Extracts from "A Nation of Mrs. Slipslops" by Honor Tracy

The days are long past when Greek or Latin verses flowed from the lips of our national leaders, but now they appear to lack the most elementary common knowledge. Hardly a week goes by without a bloomer that once would have provoked hilarity in the Lower Fourth, and no one seems to notice. And the guilty are not anxious young students, with nothing in mind but a degree and a clerking job to follow, but figures in public life, writers and speakers, academics, the intelligentsia.

I have written before of the gruesome pronunciation and wanton changing of stress that are wrecking its music and rhythm, and, as if that weren't enough, words increasingly used in a sense which is quite simply wrong.

Another ominous development is the misused word which *sounds* not wholly unlike the appropriate one; thus I recently read of someone "flaunting" the Victorian code of ethics when the writer plainly meant "flouting". I have heard "contrivance" for "connivance", "contraption" for "contraction", "refrain" for "restrain"; and an interviewer on B.B.C. television describe the requisites for a game as the "impedimenta". At least, I think that was what he said unless he had an implement in his speech.

I have often puzzled as to what that weary old phrase "play it by ear" could mean, and this may well be it. And it strikes me as ominous because it seems to suggest that people no longer read, but acquire a vocabulary, as Mrs. Slipslop did, by listening to the spoken word and getting it wrong.

If nothing is done to rectify matters, mistakes will harden into usage and we shall find them in the next edition of the O.E.D. For by some pundits today, those who imagine all trends to be wholesome merely because they occur, usage is revered as a sacred cow. Cowish it may be, but sacred it is not.

Those who promote it are of a piece with artists who will not learn to draw, composers who reject the theory of music in order to give their "inspiration" a freer run. We know the grisly outcome of that, but frivolity over words will have consequences graver still. As a child I was taught that speech was given by God to draw men together. We should beware lest one of these days we shan't have an earthly what anyone else is trying to say.